BUILDING MUSCLE

Life Is Your Trainer

2nd Edition

Written by

Nathan W. Evans, Jr.

Dedication

Robert Evans and Maxine Wright (Pop Pop & Grandmother). Thank you for your love and guidance. You both where the glue that kept our family together and I thank you both for the values and lessons you taught me. I'm proud to use what you taught me to succeed in life and pass it down to my own family in the near future.

Nathan Evans Sr. and Kathleen Dorris (Dad & Mom) I love you for being the ones who brought me to life. Thanks for having the courage to raise and deal with me. I know it wasn't easy, but your hard work paid off, and you created a blessing for the world.

I will always love you: Joshua and Joziah (Brothers) Jaelynn (Niece) Josh Jr. (Nephew)

Ladies of my life: Tamaira Mortimore (Fiancée), Ashley Dorris & Natasha Squair

Acknowledgments

Thanks to my brother, best friend and business partner Les Squair Jr. for being one of my biggest supporters and mentors. I love you bro. Thank you to my brothers David Ruiz, Tony Chatman, Ty Lewis and Kevin Adorno, for your constant love and support. You guys encouraged and empowered me during some of the most challenging times in my life, and I owe you all for that.

To Danielle Jones, Natasha Squair, and Torey Jones, I thank you, ladies, for always being supportive of me and genuinely spreading your love with me.

Thank you to the cities of Pleasantville and Atlantic City for raising me and allowing me to give back to my communities.

To my long-distance mentors Inky Johnson, Dr. Eric Thomas, Carlas Quinney Jr, and Will Smith, thank you for living out your purpose and inspiring me to NEVER QUIT on my dreams and goals. My family's future has been blessed because of your influence.

Contents

A Message for the Reader
You Are Not Alone

"What happens when you spend your entire life trying to be someone, but you never become that person? What happens when you're physically alive to everyone else but dead to yourself? What happens when you become numb to pain, do you even acknowledge the effects of it?" These were all the questions that I began asking myself when I finally accepted that my dream of playing professional basketball had ended.

Since I was a young kid, I had invested my time and energy into becoming the best basketball player that I could be. What started as a love for the game at the innocent age of two years old became a burning passion and a very detailed dream to get my Mother out of our poverty struct, gang-affiliated, roach-infested environment. Even though I was only two years old when my parents purchased me my first "Fisher-Price" basketball court, I remember it like it was yesterday. Shoe boxes filled with old photos also helped me recall a lot of my old childhood memories which my Dad kept in his basement. As you can probably tell, we were far from wealthy, hell we were far from the middle class in the eyes of society. For a large chunk of my childhood, I ate oodles & noodles, peanut butter & jelly sandwiches, microwavable chicken nuggets and tuna melts. School lunches helped from time to time, but most of the time the food was garbage a.k.a. boiled hot-dogs and sauerkraut. These weren't necessarily ideal conditions, but we made it work.

Basketball kept me out of a lot of trouble that so many people in my neighborhood couldn't avoid. While friends of mine were chasing girls, doing drugs, or selling drugs, I was pounding my Spalding basketball on the elevated pavement of our housing complexes basketball court. The neighborhood OG's and gang members somewhat protected me as they would never allow me to even get close to drugs and anything else they may have been involved in. I have seen this as their way of showing to me. I began to understand that because I was talented at basketball, they kept trouble away from me or at least what they could control. The people who were initiated into that lifestyle didn't necessarily have the talent that I did so they brought them into the street life. If you weren't hooping or an honor student you were a drug dealer or user. That was how the hood operated.

As my basketball skills increased, my life became more difficult to deal with mentally. Money, or should I say the lack thereof began to tear my family apart. It seemed like every day, my Mother was stressed over bills. Every piece of mail that came to our house seemed to bring more anxiety and anger to her. All I saw was anguish, and all I wanted to do was to help. I couldn't understand why we were struggling so much? I would have sold drugs, but the thought of my parents' disappointment felt worst than the possibility of getting caught and going to jail.

Even though I was in my local press newspaper every week for basketball, I was in my room crying every week as well from managing the trauma of my life outside of school. Mentally, I was weak and broken. Externally I was the man, all-star athlete, prom king and even most likely to be famous as voted by my peers. No one knew what I really thought about myself. No one knew the self-dialogue I would have with my self. This was my reality preceding the time frame that I discuss in this book. I'm telling you this to set the tone before you dive in. I was great at making my life look beautiful, even though it was extremely ugly at times.

Here's the thing; this story isn't just my story. This is the story of so many of our young Kings and Queens who suffer mentally from defining themselves by what they have done and not who they currently are and what they can be. This is OUR story, these are OUR struggles, and now it's time to own OUR greatness.

Stage 1:

"Reality Check"

I once heard something extremely profound during a conference where Inky Johnson spoke at, and that was this, "the biggest mistake is that people think where they meet you is where you've always been."

"Despite what most people may believe about me, I started my journey weakly and small, and I don't mean just in the physical sense.

If I told you I was poor for a large percentage of my life, would you believe me?

If I told you I grew up in the hood surrounded by drugs, gun violence, and prostitution, would you believe me?

If I told you I finished high school with a full ride to play division II basketball and left after my first semester would you believe me?

If I told I went to 5 different colleges after that, would you believe me?

If I told you my family and I were evicted from our home when I decided to come home from school, would you believe me?

If I've told you I hurt multiple women in my life by being young-minded, would you believe me?

If I told you that my parents and I are just starting to really build our relationships, would you believe me?

If I told you that who you assume I am is more than likely wrong, would you believe me?

All of these trials in my life came to break me and make me quit. However, I persevered once I realized that my life was not just about me but about those around me. My family, those who may have been going through similar situations as myself, the next generation coming behind me, this was what my life was about.

All of these things, I just spoke of transpired because I only was thinking of myself. I had no external motivation or a reason for what I was doing. I operated off of my feelings, and as a result I hit some of the lowest points in my life.

Something positive did come from all of this pain and suffering. I began to get bigger and stronger physically, mentally, and spiritually.

I started to master the art of BUILDING MUSCLE. The thing about BUILDING MUSCLE is this; you should never stop.

There is always room to become stronger and better, and with life as your trainer you can either quit when the pressure is on you or use that pressure to grow and get stronger."

Instead of saying I have to do this, I have to do that, start saying I'm blessed to do this, I'm blessed to do that.

We must first change our perspective about life if we aspire to be truly happy. By now I'm sure we all know the power of energy. Think of your thoughts as the battery for your day, which eventually is what enhances your week, months, years and ultimately the rest of your life. If those batteries are plugged into a positive mindset productive actions will follow. The old cliché that thoughts become things is true.

Here is my journey on how I built muscle through the constant weight that life put on me. My goal is not to teach you some secret plan or give you new concepts but to tell you what worked for me during my times of adversity that made me into the Man I am today. Let's build muscle together. It's time to train!

Training Session 1:
Emergency Trip

"Life is going to punch you in the face!"

~ Andy Frisella

"Josh call dad and tell him to meet us at the hospital!" "Hopefully we don't get pulled over."

I had no idea where my license was, but at the same time, I didn't care. I just needed to get my Pop Pop to the hospital as fast as possible. He was extremely stubborn, but I could tell that he was in a massive amount of pain. His face mimicked someone being pierced with a knife in their stomach. I decided and made the executive decision to take him to the hospital. My brother Josh and I grabbed him off the couch where he'd been sitting all day in pain, and we forced him to get in his van. Josh strapped his seatbelt on as I ran back in to grab his wallet.

"I think we have everything, call dad and tell him we are on our way to the hospital with Pop Pop!"

"He didn't answer," Josh said.

I sped through every light until I reached the parkway, that was when I really floored the gas peddle. My dad called my phone back minutes later, and Josh put him on speaker.

"Booman! What's wrong?" My dad was one of the few people who still called me by my nickname. At the moment I didn't know what was wrong I just knew it was serious.

"I don't know, but Pop Pop looks really bad, so we decided to take him to the emergency room, can you meet us here?"

"I'm leaving now," my dad said in a frantic voice.

Once we reached the hospital, we quickly rushed him in the emergency room for help. The doctor took my Pop Pop to the back right before my dad arrived.

My dad came rushing in short of breath.

"Booman what happened?"

"I don't know, I came into the house, and he looked like he was in pain. He was holding his stomach and sweating. Josh said he's been like that for a few hours, so I panicked and brought him here."

Just about an hour later, the doctor came out to speak with us.

"Are you Robert's family?"

"Yes, Doc, what's going on, is he ok?" my dad said.

The doctor responded with uncertainty, "We ran a few tests on him, and we found what is called gangrene within his gut."

I didn't know much about gangrene, but I knew it wasn't good.

"So, what does that mean?" I said.

"Gangrene is a disease that occurs when blood tissue dies. This can be the cause of an injury which could have triggered an infection. We will run a few more tests on him to see how severe it is, and then we will be able to know how we can treat this condition or if we can treat it at all."

I didn't like the doctor's second response at all. As the doctor left my dad began calling his brothers and sisters to meet us at the hospital. I really hate the feeling of uncertainty. My nerves always seem to get the best of me, so I decided to take a walk down the hallway.

I just graduated high school two months before this day, and I hadn't gone to church or prayed for months before my graduation. All I cared about during that time frame was basketball and girls. Despite my absence from church and lack of prayer I knew it wouldn't hurt to ask for God's help in this situation. I didn't want anyone to see me praying, so I turned to the closest window and said in a low tone

"I know we haven't spoken too much lately, but I really need your help. God please let my Pop Pop walk out of this situation healthy, please! Amen."

I didn't know what else to say at the moment. About thirty-five minutes later my aunt and uncles came rushing in. My family didn't really get along too well at all, so there was an unsettling tension in the room. We waited for just about three hours before doctors came out again. During that time my family barely spoke, everyone pretty much kept their distance except me, my dad and my brother Josh. I was kind of annoyed that my family couldn't settle their differences during a time like this, but I didn't try to ease the tension neither.

After waiting anxiously for roughly three hours, the doctor finally came back out, but this time, his face showed no signs of optimism. All the tension that was previously in the room was gone at this point, and it was replaced with a sense of worry.

"So any good news doctor?" My dad said in an uneasy voice.

The doctor paused for a brief second, took a deep breath and said "so we ran a few more tests on Robert and I'm sorry to inform you that the gangrene has spread and has begun to eat away at Robert's internal organs."

My heart dropped instantly, and I felt sick. "so what can you do? What treatment does he need doctor!?" I said in a frantic voice.

Again the doctor paused. "Unfortunately, the gangrene is to a level of severity that treatment cannot fix. As of right now Robert is on a ventilator and may have a few more days to live. Being that the tubes are running through his mouth, he is unable to speak, but he can hear you. I'm extremely sorry about this news."

All of the sounds in the room were sucked out and replaced with dead silence. One tear came out my right eye then another out of my left eye; seconds later my cheeks were filled with tears. My aunt Chastity broke down in the corner as my uncle went to comfort her and my dad still wore a shocked look on his face before eventually tearing up. So many different things were running through my head at this moment. Was this really the last time that I would see my Pop-Pop, someone I looked up to? Someone who played a major role in raising me to become the man I am today. He was my best friend and supported me in everything that I did from academics to sports, to me getting my first job and my license. I never wanted for anything when my Pop-Pop was around.

Three weeks before this day, my Pop-Pop told me that he would drive me to school in Memphis, Tennessee where I had received a scholarship to play basketball at a Division II school called Lemoyne-Owen College. I planned on flying, but he was so excited that he insisted on driving me there from New Jersey. We had the whole trip planned out; we would make a few stops along the way to visit a few places and still make it to the college early for me to get settled in.

My Pop-Pop would brag to all of his friends on Cedar Lane about how his grandson was going away to college. My dad and mom never graduated from high school, and neither did he, so the fact that I had done that and was going to college was the largest accomplishment ever to him. It was actually overwhelming for me. I was the first person in my immediate family to leave for school, and I knew that I had an opportunity to change the blueprint for my family.

Being back and forth in the hospital every day caused me to lose all sight of college. It was the last thing that I could think of. The doctor allowed us to go three people at a time into the back room that my Pop-Pop was being treated in. My dad, my brother and I went back together. My dad walked in first while my brother and I followed. I began to feel weak as I looked at my Pop Pop. Tubes were all over the place, two in his nose and one lodged into his mouth. His face was sunken and skinny, his eyes were glassy, and he had a look in them as if he wasn't ready to die. My heart felt so broken, and I couldn't stop crying as I gave my best friend a kiss on his forehead. I felt empty as if the doctor just took my heart out and I had a blank look on my face as I reminisced the happiest moment I shared with my Pop-Pop knowing that we wouldn't be able to create more of those memories, and that was killing me. As he closed his eyes one last time I felt like part of me died with him. My dad took my brother and me out of the room as Josh was crying hysterically. The rest of my family that showed up would take their turns going back to see my Pop Pop one more time. After everyone had their chance to see him the doctor came out one last time.

"Evans family, again I am truly sorry about this very unfortunate situation. My condolences are with you all."

He paused for a brief moment and then said, "If everyone has had their chance to see Robert we will be proceeding with the process of taking out the ventilator. Again we are sorry about your loss and our condolences are with you all."

Key #1 To Building Muscle:

You Can't Skip Adversity You Can Only Learn From It

Training Session 2:
Family Feud

"We all lose when the family feuds"

~ Jay-Z

Moments after the doctor left the room; I could hear my aunt yelling and cursing at my dad and uncles. The blame game began immediately, and everyone was at each other's neck for a situation that was no one's fault. I couldn't believe what I was hearing and seeing. I was seconds from losing it and snapping on everyone before my dad told my brother and me to come on and we left the hospital. How could everyone act like this?

How could we not be comforting each other right now?

How would my Pop Pop feel right now if he could see us?

That drive from the hospital was a long and quiet one. I couldn't believe that I wouldn't be able to speak with my Pop-Pop again. It felt so unreal.

Plans for the funeral were arranged the day after and we decided to meet as a family at my Pop Pop's house since that was where mostly everyone was raised, including his grandkids. We had a lot of families come from out of town, but I was excited most to see my cousins from Detroit. It was always a good time when they were in town and out of all of my cousins I was closer to them than everyone else even though we didn't see each other often. I don't really think my Pop-Pop being gone really hit anyone that first week until the actual funeral. To my surprise, we actually acted like a tight nit family until the day after the funeral once everyone started making their way back to my Pop-Pop's house and for dinner that night. Shortly after that tensions picked back up and the battle over his house and cars began. It was like everyone wanted his possessions for selfish reasons. Everyone wanted to feel as if their relationship with him was closer than anyone else.

Fast forward to the present day, the fighting amongst everyone has stopped, but the tension can still be felt. It's as if he was the glue that held everyone together and since he was gone all the pieces fell apart. Even though I never got involved with my families drama I did have some demons of my own that I battled with. I spent countless nights out drinking and partying after my Pop-Pop's funeral. I thought this would be a good way to cope with my pain. I had roughly a week before I would have to leave for school and I made everyday count, literally partying and alcohol every day. I started living in those dark moments, and it was hurting me emotionally. I never gave myself a chance to heal and morn, and that became a major issue. I didn't speak to God during this time, and honestly I was angry at God and everyone else around me for no reason. Life wasn't fair in my eyes, but at that time I failed to realize that life wasn't fair for anyone so complaining was pointless.

Key #2 To Building Muscle:

Don't Waste Time Trying To Avoid Pain But Instead Embrace It.

Training Session 3:
Always In My Heart

"I ain't trying to rock no shirts that say "in memory"
I'm praying that he makes it, wishin' we could go back
cause honestly all the times that we had those be the
best memories..."

~ Big Sean

A few days before my flight to leave for Memphis, I started having dreams about my Pop-Pop taking me down to school. I would literally wake up with cold sweats. It hadn't really hit me yet that he was gone but not seeing him in the living room with his feet up made me feel uncomfortable. Imagine being with your best friend one day then losing him the next, that's how I felt. He was much more than my dad's father; he was my mentor and best friend. I never learned from him because he sat me down and taught me lessons but instead I learned from his actions and how he carried himself as a man. Watching him day in and day out showed me what hard work looked like. No, he didn't go to college, hell he didn't even finish high school, he didn't own his own company or make seven figures a year, but at the end of the day, he was a

MAN. He did whatever it took to provide for his family and make sure that my dad, uncles, and aunt didn't lack anything. He was a blue-collar guy; he worked, he cleaned the house, mowed the lawn, fixed cars, kept food on the table and supported his kids and grandkids. He was a real man who never made an excuse or asked for a handout despite his lack of education and resources. He didn't operate off of his feelings, he just did what needed to be done and some. Even though I was a kid I was observing and soaking up all these values like a sponge on a wet counter.

It didn't matter to me how much money I made in the future, what kind of career I had or where I lived, I knew I had one job to do, and that was to be a real man like him. A man that would love and care for his family so much that he would grind endlessly to provide for them. I keep an old picture of myself and my Pop Pop in my wallet from Christmas when I was two years old as a daily reminder to myself of his love for me and also the legacy I needed to continue building.

A couple of days before I left for Memphis, Tennessee I would go to get a chest piece tattoo that reads "ALWAYS IN MY HEART POP-POP" along with his birthdate and the day he passed. This was my way of having a constant reminder of where my Pop-Pop was no matter where I went. I had three tattoos previous to this, and I never got one because I wanted to be cool. Each one had its own significant meaning behind it, and this was my way of expression and reminding myself of my blessings. I now represented something much bigger than myself, but life would constantly try to make me forget that.

Key #3 To Building Muscle:

Focus On What And Who You Represent. You Will Let Yourself down If You're Only Focused on Yourself.

Stage 1 Review:

"Reality checks come at the most unexpected times. You really can never be prepared for them, but you can learn from them."

Keys To Building Muscle #1-3:

1. You Can't Skip Adversity You Can Only Learn From It.

2. Don't Waste Time Trying To Avoid Pain But Instead Embrace It.

3. Focus On What And Who You Represent. You Will Let Yourself Down If You're Only Focused On Yourself.

Stage 2:

"Hitting a Plateau"

The first mistake most people make during the process of building the life of their dreams is thinking that they won't face obstacles. To believe that you won't run into a brick wall on your way to your goals is not only naïve but a sure fired way to ensure that you will never reach them.

Nothing great in life was ever achieved without struggle. That struggle can range from starting your first business to having a baby for women. You will go through pain before the beauty of your decisions reveals itself.

Hitting a plateau is mandatory, but how you progress through that plateau is what will determine how your life will pan out. You will either become motivated by the bumps in the road to get to your destination, or you will become discouraged and turn around.

This phase in life is where I learned my most valuable lessons and ultimately learned that I have no control over my struggles; I just control how I learn from them.

Training Session 4:
Environment Change

"What you allow will continue"

~ Unknown

I could have easily stayed home for college, but I needed an environment change badly after my Pop-Pop's passing, and Memphis was just far enough for me to make that change. My parents never went to college let alone graduated high school. I didn't have much of an example to follow when it came to that, but because they never experienced college or high school graduation for that matter I felt as if I had to do it. I had to set the standard for what would be expected from our family for the future.

I used my talents in basketball to parlay a full athletic scholarship to a Division II school in Memphis, Tennessee called Lemoyne-Owen College. The school allowed me to arrive at class a week late because of my Pop-Pop's funeral service. My dad and mom ended up splitting the payment for my flight to Memphis, Tennessee despite really having the funds to send me. I'd never actually flown in a plane before, and this wouldn't only be my first time, but I also would be flying alone to a city where I knew no one. My mom dropped me off at the Philadelphia airport and just like most mothers she was nervous about letting me go that far especially all alone.

"Thanks mom, I love you" I said.

"Booman, do you have everything?" she said in a frantic tone.

"Yes mom."

"Did you pack all of your underwear?"

"Yes mom," I said in an annoyed voice.

"Don't forget to call me as soon as you land!"

"I won't mom, I promise"

"Booman! Did you remember your ID?!"

"Yes mom, I have everything."

Any more of this going back and forth and I was bound to miss my flight. She finally gave me a hug and a kiss as I rushed to my gate.

I'll be honest; I was pretty nervous because I wasn't sure what to expect. A friend of mine told me to chew gum during the takeoff of the flight so my ears wouldn't pop so I chewed four pieces of gum since my nerves were really bad. That was probably much more than I needed at the time, but I didn't care.

During the flight, all I could think about was my Pop Pop saying "I'll drive you to school." I didn't know how to stomach seeing him in that hospital bed helpless. He was always one of the strongest men I knew, someone I looked up to because of his work ethic to support his family. I hoped that school and basketball would distract me from this situation and ease my pain a little. I guess I would see once I got there.

The head coach of Lemoyne-Owen men's basketball team picked me up from the airport. As we drove to campus, he gave me condolences for my Pop-Pop, and he gave me a little history lesson on Memphis and what it used to be. In a way it was difficult for me to picture what he was describing because of the amount of abandoned buildings and ghettos I had seen. The history that he spoke of about Memphis was unbelievable; you would never know that some of the most historic moments in jazz, pop music and black history took place there. We pulled up to the campus, and it was far from what I expected. I was use to visiting nice universities, and even when I looked up this school online the pictures seemed decent. They obviously caught all the nice buildings for photos and disregarded the rest of the campus. The team's assistant coach took me to my dorm room after showing me the gym.

The campus had one set of dorms, and they were apartment-style. It reminded me of home because it looked very similar to Woodlyn Avenue projects where I lived for majority of my life. My roommate Rasheed was a senior and captain of the men's basketball team. I was actually surprised that I was his roommate since I was a freshman. The assumption was that I would room with other freshman, but this living arrangement later showed it's perks.

That first night on campus was a night that I would never forget. Rasheed took me to Beale Street and if you've ever been to Memphis, Tennessee then you've heard of Beale Street.

Beale Street is a street in Memphis that turns into one massive party at night with its bars and clubs. I was 18 years old at the time, and you had to be 21 years old to even get on the street, but Rasheed managed to get me there and into a night club that was 21+. This club was like nothing I had experienced at home. I was exposed to so much already and the night just started. There was a stage with half-naked girls on it and most of them I recognized from campus that same day. We had our own V.I.P. section with a few of the men's basketball team players from other colleges in the area. All I could think while partying in our section was that I could live like this. I was certain that this was what college was about; go to class, play ball and party.

I had been in Memphis all of twelve hours, and I was loving it. This was the environmental change that I needed, or at least that was what I thought. After partying for about an hour I had already taken three shots of tequila, had a cup of cranberry & vodka, and I was drunk and acting like a cool guy. I would occasionally drink back at home with my friends but nothing like this. I felt as if I was in the matrix, well that was until a massive fight broke out in the section next to us. This situation turned into an all-out brawl, I'm talking WWF Royal Rumble style fight. Rasheed pushed me from behind and said "let's go!" as we ran towards the nearest emergency exit on the side of the club. As the club emptied out the brawl made its way to the parking lot. There were so many people fighting that I couldn't tell who was against who. Just about a minute after that gunshots began to ring within the scuffle. Instantly we scattered and following the shots were police sirens.

Myself and Rasheed ran about seven blocks at least before we stopped to breathe. With my heart racing and sweat pouring down my face, my perspective of what I previously thought about Memphis changed, and it started reminding me of home and all the violence in my own hood. I thought I was getting away from these type of situations coming out here, but it was as if I never left my old environment.

"You good?" Rasheed said.

"Yeah I'm cool," I responded.

Even if I was scared or nervous, I wasn't going to admit it. I did know however where not to go when it came to hanging out anymore.

Key #4 To Building Muscle:

Avoid Negative Energy At All Costs

Training Session 5
Quitting Is a Dangerous Option

"It's always too early to quit"

~ Norman Vincent Peale

The next day we joked about the night before over lunch as if it was actually funny. Also, today would be my first collegiate basketball practice. I never bothered to look online at the roster to at least see what my teammates looked like because honestly I didn't care. My attitude was way past confident and knocking on the door of cockiness when it came to basketball. The age difference between myself and some of my teammates had to be roughly 6-8 years. I was literally playing on a team full of grown men. In a way it was intimidating, but my attitude wouldn't let me show it, and I also was determined to make a name for myself. A month later we had our first scrimmage of the season which was against Lane College. For the earlier portions of the game I didn't see the floor since I was a freshman. I sat there on the bench anxious to play. With three minutes left in the first half I finally got subbed in. My first offensive play of the game came from a steal where I had pickpocketed the shooting guard on the other team and was in the clear for a fast break dunk. My cockiness set in an I didn't take the easy basket on the fast break, but instead I shot and made a 3 pointer. My coach wasn't impressed at all. I would eventually end the game on what I thought was a high note with 11 points which was more than any other freshmen and even some of the upperclassmen had. I felt as if I had solidified my spot on the team and that I would get quality playing time during the season. My coach had a different thought in mind. In his eyes I showed flashes of being arrogant and the inability to be a team player from my actions within the game and practices to come.

Things only got worse as time went on, and most of my issues occurred off the court. I started to become that person that I was before I came to Memphis right after my Pop-Pop passed away. Quiet and laid back is my demeanor now but that was the last thing I was on campus. I thought that I was the turn-up king! I was at every party and function on campus. I literally didn't miss anything from dorm parties to probates. For some reasons the girls on campus loved guys from up north and I was from New Jersey, so I took advantage of that. I spent more time with girls than my actual teammates. I would go from class to a girls room, to practice back to another girls room, to dinner back to another girls room. Honestly looking back on my actions now I have no idea what I was thinking. I can barely recognize the person that I'm telling you about.

It wasn't until my grades came in where reality started to hit me. Our progress reports were sent to our coach to see where the team stood academically. I had been an "A/B" student my entire life, so to have anything under that was unacceptable. My grades not only came back below average but for the first time in my life I was failing a class. I felt my emotions go from a natural high to a downward spiral. I made the mistake of committing to being a business major which I had no interest in. I only chose it because it sounded respectable when people would ask me what my major was and I assumed that it was the major people pursued to get a "good job." I didn't know that I had a worker bee mindset and I wasn't thinking for or about myself and the outcome I would produce. I was working hard to be an average worker at best without even knowing it.

My mother was the type of mother that was always concerned with how I was doing, which I saw as annoying during that time. Every few days or so she would call and ask me "how school was going and how were my grades?" I would lie every week and say "everything is going great!" because I knew what she expected and I didn't want to disappoint her. After those phone calls I would get back to being unproductive. I brushed off the grades as if they didn't matter and I kept doing what I was doing which was partying, hanging out until the morning, drinking and messing with different girls. I hadn't been knocked down enough yet to want to change my behaviors.

A couple of weeks before our first regular-season home game opener our men's basketball team was invited to a banquet dinner in honor of a previous Hall of Fame coach from Lemonye-Owen College who was also a major public figure within the city of Memphis. This night at the banquet would make me realize how irresponsibly I had been living the past few months. John Calipari who is the head coach of the University of Kentucky now but at this time was the head coach for the University of Memphis spoke in honor of the Hall of Fame coach at dinner. He gave a lot of praise while on the podium, but he said something profound that would stick with this 18-year-old kid from New Jersey forever.

"The only way to win on the court and in life is to make your life about someone else and not yourself. You'll keep going when adversity hits you if someone depends on you."

As simple and as short of a statement that was, it hit a trigger in my mind and I started to look at my actions during my time in Memphis. I was the most selfish version of myself possible. I didn't care what my coach thought, my professors thought or even what my parents thought. I had anger and bitterness within my heart, and I wanted to fill that void where happiness and purpose supposed to be. I was focused solely on myself, and as a result I didn't work hard for anything. I acted as if I was a privileged kid as if someone owed me something. I walked around campus like I was untouchable. My grades were a reflection of my poor efforts as well as my actions on the court. I was far from a team player, and it affected me the most.

I would soon be served a slice of humble pie as the season kicked into high gear and my playing time was decreased significantly. I felt like I didn't deserve to sit on the bench as a freshman as if I didn't have to pay my dues. I began to get frustrated and annoyed. I remember thinking that I should be playing on television at a major university. I believed that I was above the program and deserved the red carpet treatment. I'm not sure why I thought this way because I never acted this way on my high school team or AAU team and I was an All-Star then. If anything that was the time to be cocky when I was dominating. It was like I was becoming a new person. A person that I didn't like, a person who was arrogant, lazy and privileged. Why should I have something that I didn't work for? What gave me the right to think like this? When December came around I began to fall into a very deep depression. I had dug myself into a whole academically, my confidence on the court hit a low and I felt as if I was letting my Pop-Pop down not to mention that me messing with girls on campus was ruining my relationship with my girlfriend at home. Yes I will be the first to admit that I was extremely wrong and selfish for stringing her along while I acted like a dog at school, I wasn't myself. I began to hate myself, and I was all alone even when I wasn't alone. I was in desperate need of some serious guidance in my life.

Three days before my birthday on December 10th, I decided to meet with my coach to tell him that I wouldn't be returning for the spring semester. I had a lot of demons that were holding me back at home that needed to be dealt with and I knew I could be of no service to the program under these conditions. That and my grades wouldn't have been good enough to play during the next semester anyway. I had to get back to the person I once was, the person my Pop Pop was proud to brag to his friends about. The person, my parents, loved and raised to do the right things and walk with character. Right before I left the office my coach had told me that I had the highest scholarship offer in terms of money given on the team, but he respected my decision and wished me the best. I couldn't believe I was throwing all of this away. How could he drop a bomb on me like that as if I didn't feel bad enough. I had a scholarship that people would kill for and I threw it away. I felt like a quitter and a loser and to be honest at that time I was both.

Key #5 To Building Muscle:

QUIT QUITTING. "QUITTERS never win, and WINNERS never quit."

Training Session 6:
Professional failure

*"Your Muscle has to be pushed to the point
of failure; it needs to be pushed constantly"*

~ Kev Decor

After staying home and working for a few months, I decided that it was time for me to get back in school. This time around would be much more difficult than my initial experience in Memphis because I no longer had a full athletic scholarship. I was now starting from scratch with no money, no idea of what school I would attend and I had to search for scholarships, apply for loans and get financial aid. I got accepted to a few schools, and I was determined to get some redemption for myself. However for some reason no matter what school I attended I just couldn't find my place. I bounced around from school to school for almost three years and made no progress. I ended up right where I first started every time at home. I literally traveled from coast to coast searching for a situation that would work for me. I went to schools as far as New Mexico looking for my perfect fit. As I continued to fail at finding a comfortable fit I started to feel as though school wasn't for me anymore. My confidence made a significant decrease once again, and my dreams of playing professional basketball were crumbling right before my eyes. Nothing was working for me and I made numerous excuses on why each situation wasn't the right situation. I couldn't help but to feel like a failure. I wasn't good at succeeding in school, but I was a professional at failing in life. Man if they only gave awards for failing I would have been a 4x champ. It was as if my life was making the same repeating cycle. I had hit a brick wall as far as my options, and I had no idea how to get over the hump.

My Pop-Pop and my father both wanted me to live a better life than they lived, but during this time I feared that I would live a life of far less significance than them. My depression continued to grow, and I spent many nights crying with tears of disappointment. I remember as a kid being asked about my future goals for when I would become an adult. My response was always,

"I'm going to be playing in the NBA, and I'm going to take care of my family with the money."

I wish I could have gone back to that kid and apologized for failing him. I was nothing like that version of myself that I thought I would be. That kid was ambitious, optimistic, and had a vision. I had become the complete opposite and in a fight to succeed I was down 0-2. I would later in life learn the importance of failing in regards to learning and succeeding.

Key #6 To Building Muscle:

Professional Failures Are Some Of The Most Successful People On Earth Because They've Mastered The Art Of Learning And Applying The Knowledge Gathered From Failing.

Stage 2 Review:

Plateaus are temporary destinations for you to check your progress and analyze your next move.

Keys To Building Muscle #4-6

1. Avoid Negative Energy At All Costs

2. Quit Quitting, Quitters Never Win, And Winners Never Quit

Professional Failures Are Some Of The Most Successful People On Earth Because They've Mastered The Art Of Learning And Applying The Knowledge Gathered From Failing.

Stage 3:

"Self-Assessment"

I want to challenge you to assess yourself daily, I challenge you to be bluntly honest with yourself every day.

If every morning when you went to the mirror in your bathroom and could speak with a younger version of yourself what would you say or show them to make them excited to live your life in the future?

What would their facial expressions say to you?

Would they be excited to be you?

Would they be disappointed at where you are in life?

Assess yourself every morning when you wake up and also before you go to bed at night. Look in the mirror and talk to yourself. Is that younger version of yourself satisfied with your production during that day?

Remember you won't satisfy yourself every day, but if that younger version of yourself can see that you are giving maximal effort to make their future better then they will accept your flaws.

Training Session 7:

My Biggest Regret

"You love me, and I love you, and your heart hurts, and
mines does too, and it's just words, and they cut deep, but it's
our world, it's just us two"

~ Drake

"I hate living here, man I don't care none of us are going to live together anymore anyway!"

Those words I still wish I could take back to this day. My mother broke down in tears after that and ran into her bedroom and slammed the door. I realized that I made the biggest mistake of my life, and I allowed my emotions to hurt my mom, someone who did everything she could to take care of myself, my brother and my cousins. I strongly believe that everything in life happens for a reason and there's no need for regrets, but this situation made me regret my actions. Just about two weeks before this incident my mom notified me that we were being evicted from our home. I was so caught off guard and angry. I had just came from playing basketball when she told me. I could see how difficult it was for her to tell me by the look in her eyes. She seemed very uneasy, and I could tell that she didn't want to disappoint me, but at the moment I let my feelings get the best of me and allowed my anger to take over my emotions.

"Why am I just finding out?"

"What are we supposed to do?"

"I could have worked and helped why wouldn't you tell me beforehand?"

I kept throwing frustrating questions at her, and she couldn't answer me. She just looked at me with a very defeated look on her face as if she let me down. Not once did I ask if she was ok or attempt to help her find a solution. I was extremely selfish and only thought about how this would affect me. I kept thinking about what my friends would say about me. I cared more about how things looked from the outside looking in instead of helping my mother rebound from this and finding a solution for the family.

I didn't take in to account that she was raising and supporting me, my brother, three of my younger cousins and also my grandmother and grandfather. Out of all the people in the house, she was the only one bringing in money to pay for bills and buy food. Every time I got a little bit of money I would buy food or clothes for myself, but I didn't offer to buy food for the house. I only cared about my needs and wants.

The tension in the house grew as it got closer to our eviction date. Where we would live and if we would all still live together was uncertain. My new girlfriends older brother came to help us pack up during our final night at the house. Everyone had found somewhere to stay whether that had been with family or friends. As we continued to pack up the U-HAUL, I began to get frustrated with loading the truck. It was just so much stuff from couches to little nicknacks in boxes. My mother was a lot more frustrated than me, but she held her composure well. That was until I started arguing with my brother because he was moving too slow. She broke her silence and snapped,

"Shut up and come on!"

"This isn't even my stuff," I said.

"I don't care, pick it up, and come on!"

I started to go off on a tantrum, and then I said those words that I will never forget.

"I hate living here, man I don't care none of us are going to live together anymore anyway!"

A dead silence came over the house, and it was as if I pierced her heart with a sword. She paused and broke down into tears, ran in her room and slammed the door. I can't imagine how low she felt. She was under so much pressure, and I kicked her while she was down. She was losing her home and had no means to provide for us anymore, and I made it worse. I knew she was hurt and I added to that hurtful disappointing feeling by pushing her back down when she tried to get up. I immediately realized what I did, but I didn't know how to apologize, and it was too late, that damage had been done already. It honestly wouldn't have helped during that moment anyway. I had never seen her in this state of pain and disappointment. How could I be so ungrateful and ignorant?

That moment has haunted me since then and still slight hurts till this day. I had hurt my mom bad, and I couldn't take back what I said. Man if you could only see the look in her eyes, it was as if she lost some of her life. I was her first son, and she looked at me as if I was a murderer. I can't explain the degree to how much pain I caused her during that moment. As time went past and we all settled into other homes over the next few months that image kept playing in my head. After about four months I finally gathered the courage to apologize. I believe by me saying what I said that day hurt me more than it hurt her.

Often the memories of our eviction back on West Mulberry Avenue resurfaced. When we initially all separated, I helped my mom move her stuff to my aunts' house in Newtonville, so I assumed she had been living there. What I found out was that my mom was there for a very little period of time and that she ended up living in a motel with my baby brother for a few weeks. This news brought tears to my eyes and guilt to my heart. How could I talk to her the way I did? Why was I not in a better position to help her?

Thinking of that moment to this day almost bring tears to my eyes. She deserved the world, and I didn't have enough money even to get her lunch. I was so disappointed in myself for not being a better son. Instead of comforting her I shunned her. I couldn't imagine how she had been feeling during that time with my baby brother and no security. I vowed ever since then to treat my mother like the queen she was, and I also made a promise to myself to make sure she experienced life far beyond her previous reality. I owed it to her. I owed it to her to go as hard as I could every single day to reach my goals. I had to achieve what I believed to be success, it wasn't optional, and it still isn't. She needed a return for her investment in me. Still haunted by those harsh words I said today I just want to say that I'm sorry mom and I love you so much.

When it came to my self-assessing myself over time I realized that my life wouldn't become better until I came to grips with all the hurt and anguish from my past. I was unhappy with myself, and that's why I lashed out at my mother. She did all that she could, and I was forced to dig deep for some self-healing. The red light and loud alarm that woke me up was after that time of eviction when I was contemplating suicide. I grew up in the church since I was a baby, but I didn't feel like God cared for me at all. I had the reverse Midas Touch. Everything I touched and involved myself in didn't turn to gold but instead blew up in my face, and ultimately, I failed. I remember writing some notes during that dark time that turned into a spoken word piece that I never performed. In this manuscript will be my only time sharing these thoughts with the public:

"Who do you turn to when you have nobody? The complications of this world are eating you alive and insane is an understatement of your feelings, you look to correlate a problem with no solution and you've gotten to the point where no ones advice is good enough, because if it was, you wouldn't be tying the belt to the ceiling fan and grabbing

that chair from the kitchen, see suicide would be the easy way out and your scared as hell of the fiery home of the devil, but you figured it couldn't feel as bad as the temporary hell you've been living in, everything that once felt real feels so fake, those people you know became those people you knew, the word trust doesn't exist in your vocabulary & it feels like everyone has turned their back to you, where's your shoulder to lean on, a room full of silence never sounded so loud because as you stroll through those hallways all you can hear is voices judging you, when in reality no one's mouth is moving, you start thinking is it worth it anymore because you've lost everything and a Jordan comeback is unlikely to happen during this game of life, well unfortunately your already on your tippy toes in that chair and the leather is already around your neck, you pray God understands and forgives you for what is about to happen, and as that last tear falls from your cheek you kick the chair, as you gasp for air life becomes more clear, and you see the mistakes you made and the people you never forgave, that temporary pain is now eternal damnation, things could have been different but then you blackout, if only you could start over"

This piece came from a very dark and selfish place. I wasn't thinking of how this would affect those around me and to those people who I neglected during that time frame I ask for your forgiveness. I keep this piece in my notes because I know someone may feel the same way, and it's my responsibility to make sure that they know someone can relate to them. The difference between then and now is I stopped being selfish which ultimately saved my life and hopefully will save the lives of others.

Key #7 To Building Muscle:

Never Allow Your Emotions to Guide You

Training Session 8:
King Klev

"Even though you're gone we're still a team through your family I'll fulfill your dreams"

~ Diddy

I remember heading to Las Vegas for a professional basketball tryout to play overseas. I trained harder than I've ever trained in my life for this opportunity; I'm talking a sickening work ethic. I was so locked in on making my dream a reality that I stopped hanging with my friends because I thought they were a distraction. Despite my past situations with school and basketball, I made way for myself to be there in Vegas. I was certain that this was my ticket to my dreams. The showcase that I participated in was three games a day for two days along with skill workouts. Both days went extremely well, and I felt in my heart that I had dominated within my position against the other point guards. I was tallying up a good amount of assists, points, and rebounds per game. I was playing full-court defense and smothering my man to a point where they would get frustrated and thrown off their game.

Most importantly, I was winning games, and my team played well as a unit. We went undefeated for the two days of the showcase, and there were about thirty scouts in the building who now had seen what I could do. I even spoke with a few of them in between games in hopes of building a relationship and bettering my chances of making a roster. I was certain that my phone call would be coming in a few days for me to pack my bags and head across the waters to play ball. My dream since I was a kid was finally about to come to life. I knew that this was my purpose or so I thought.

Well, I waited by my phone and those days turned into weeks and then into months and still nothing. I didn't know what to do, and I felt as if I had exhausted all my options.

"This is where my hoop dream is ending?"

Is what I thought to myself.

I finally had been knocked down for the last time, and at that moment I gave up on my dream of being a professional athlete. I started to see life through a different lens after this experience. I started to live in the "realistic" world, and I stopped dreaming.

One day I was at my old high school playing basketball with some of my friends from around the city, and in the middle of the game I caught a glimpse of a banner hanging on the wall from my basketball teams conference championship in "07-08." I started having flashbacks of my team that year and also that time in my life. As I looked at the banner a crystal clear image of Klevins Exantus popped up in my head. Klev was a transfer from Atlantic City high school during my senior year. Klev was super confident in his abilities to play basketball at a high level, and some people thought he was overly confident and somewhat cocky because of the way he carried himself on and off the court, but honestly he did work extremely hard. I know he did because I was his training partner. When he transferred to Pleasantville High School we quickly linked and became the best guard combo in our conference.

I remember he would come to my house every morning during the summer at 7 am with two bananas in his bag, a basketball in his right hand and a gallon of water in the other hand. We trained every day for hours without fail. We would go run two miles on the high schools track every morning then head to the Pleasantville Rec Center to do skill drills and play basketball after. I couldn't even count how many games of 1-on-1 full court we played against each other. We battled like spartans. I had never come across someone so determined to succeed on the court. I didn't think anyone had me beat in that department, but I met my match. Klev had a very strong "why" as his reason for going so hard. Like most people who play basketball he had a dream to get his family out of the hood and retire his mother except unlike everyone else who just talked he was actually putting in the work to make it happen. He wasn't waking up early and training hard for fun. He had a vision of making it to the pros just like me and feeding his family with his rewards. We would go on to finish out our senior year on one of the highest notes that Pleasantville had seen since the early 2000s and we left our mark in school history. After both of us had made the Cape Atlantic All-Star team we graduated then went our separate ways once it was time to go to college. The distance got the best of our friendship, and we weren't as connected as we once were.

Just about a year or so later after I came home from my first college stop Lemonye-Owen, I received a tragic phone call that would blow my mind. I remember it like it was yesterday. It was 6:32 am when I got the call that Klev had died. I was speechless and in shock. I stayed in my room for hours thinking this had to be a dream. Nothing was making sense to me. How was it possible for someone so close to me to be gone forever. This man had so many people counting on him. He had a "why" that he could no longer serve. He literally was the link that held his family together. I did my best not to break down, but I couldn't fight the tears. The thought that you could do everything in your power to try and make a better life for your family just to lose it all in an instance scared me horribly. I already knew life was unpredictable but it never really hit me at how true that statement was until this moment.

Flashing back to that day at the gym as I looked at the conference banner and reminisced about Klev it dawned on me that I could learn from his life and how he chose to live it. See what I didn't realize back then was that Klev was in my life to teach me a lesson about the strength of your "why." He was the perfect example of someone using their "why" to keep them determined and disciplined to their craft. I personally don't think he wanted to train every day at 7 am for hours on end, but he did what he believed would take him to the next level despite his feelings. He made something out of nothing and earned a scholarship to play basketball in Texas. That opportunity wasn't looking for him; he created it; he forced it to happen. He gave himself no other options but to succeed. I wanted to honor him for teaching me this lesson through his lifestyle, so I decided to make his life and legacy a part of my "why." Even though I wasn't pursuing basketball anymore I was on another path where I needed these principles.

I still think about him to this day, and his determination lives on in me. Every time I wanted to quit what I was pursuing since that day at the gym I would picture him and me talking about how we wanted to take our families out of the hood and give our mother's the world. If I could be blessed enough to speak to Klev now I would say thank you for instilling that value in me by being an example of what sacrificing it all really meant. I miss and love you, to my friend and brother Klevins Exantus a.k.a King Klev.

Key #8 To Building Muscle:

Leave a Legacy for Others to Carry On

Training Session 9:
Making the Adjustments

"The inability to self-assess, the inability to
say where you really are who you really are,
that's a challenge for most people."

~ Dr. Eric Thomas

Years later, I found myself working in a local Vitamin Shoppe just trying to find myself as well and create some direction I'm life. I spent a lot of my time outside of the gym coping with stress at the gym. It was my peaceful place. My girlfriend always challenged me when it came to my self-development. She provided me with the external motivation that I desperately needed. She was very observant and noticed that I would work out constantly, almost like an obsession and she asked me why wasn't I trying to get paid for training others. She made a great point, but I didn't follow through with the process. I honestly didn't think much about it after she asked me. I would eventually take what she said into consideration. I remember getting so frustrated at my 9-to-5 one day to the point that I started to question myself and my complacent mindset. I began to flirt with the idea of getting certified to be a personal trainer. At first I felt uneasy because I didn't believe that my personality suited that of a personal trainer, but I would later find out that my personality was perfect for the job.

Once I decided to take the necessary steps to become a trainer, I would have an extremely slow start at gaining clients which I'm sure any new trainer does. It became frustrating, but no matter how many clients I didn't have at the time I couldn't just quit. I was a quitter for most of my life, and I didn't want to live that way anymore. Money became very tight for me while trying to train because of my lack of clientele and also my car at the time broke down. My transmission blew, and I couldn't afford to fix it. There was no way that I could take the bus to school and still make it to work on time. I had two jobs at the time, and they were too far apart in distance to chance being late by taking the bus. I was desperate and needed another vehicle fast. A week after my car broke down I was blessed with a 2015 Nissan Altima. I was back on the road, but there was still one issue, I couldn't afford my car payments.

That feeling of reality had set in again, and I knew I would have to stop training and get a second job that would pay me an hourly wage. I was so close to quitting again on something I loved doing. Even though I knew I needed a more steady income I stuck it out with my training job. I scaled back on my eating habits and started to survive off of crackers, tuna fish, rotisserie chicken, frozen vegetables and rice. My diet was horrible for someone who was training others and teaching them how to eat, but I had to survive or give in and quit training. Needless to say I made it through this rough time and maintained my car payments. I was able to get back on track with my diet, and I was able to make some good money as well all because I trusted the process. It was the first time I had done so. Before, I would quit because the process was too uncertain and too long. My lack of patience was what held me back, and I never had the chance to see what I could produce if I just stuck it out and continued to work hard. I remember calling my mom in the heat of all of this, and I told her that I thought I was going to lose my car and my job. Her first response was a scripture from the book of Matthew 6:26 that reads:

"Look at the birds; they don't plant or harvest or store food in barns, for your Heavenly Father feeds them. And aren't you far more valuable to him than they are?"

As much as I wasn't trying to hear what she was saying she was right. I had worried so much that the quality of my training was taking a hit. I was so concerned about obtaining more clients that I didn't focus on minor details of my training, and as a result I lost all of my clients.

It wasn't until I really started to take the advice my mother gave me that my career as a trainer started to take off. I got to a point where I had nothing to lose because I was already at my lowest point financially. I started to really focus on my training, and I began studying, reading books on training, watching YouTube videos and listening to podcasts. I started to apply the knowledge I learned to my own training and soon after I decided to enter my first ever men's physique show.

My purpose for prepping and participating in this show was to get myself out of my comfort zone and really challenge my discipline towards one goal. I had already seen what the process could produce with personal training, so I understood what I could produce if I didn't quit. My prep for the show was twelve weeks long, and it was one of the toughest experiences I've ever had faced mentally. The training was somewhat easy because I enjoyed working out. Maintaining my diet is what was the most difficult. Mentally it became draining, and I almost broke multiple times. I held myself accountable by inviting all of my family and friends to come see me compete. Every time that I wanted to quit I would vision all the people who said they were coming to my show calling me a liar because I didn't make good on my promise. Every week got tougher and tougher, but I finally made it to show day. Being able to step on stage and live up to my word was a huge victory for me and a major step in the right direction in regards to my discipline and mentality. I had trusted the process once again, and I was rewarded for doing so. I left out of my first ever men's physique show in 2nd place for my class and my clientele as a personal trainer was growing... My confidence in myself was rising, and this was the beginning of a positive domino effect. I never thought I would get over that hump in my life that kept me at an average standard, but I was slowly climbing my way over it.

Key #9 To Building Muscle:

Focus On What You Can Control And Keep What You Cannot Control In Your Peripheral

Stage 3 Review:

To grow as an individual, you must constantly assess your actions and behaviors so that you can make the proper adjustments to do better, and you can always do better

Keys To Building Muscle #7-9:

1. Never Allow Your Emotions To Guide You

2. Leave A Legacy For Others To Carry On

3. Focus On What You Can Control And Keep What You Cannot Control In Your Peripheral.

Stage 4:
"Progressing Over Plateaus"

The difference between people who live out their dreams and achieve their goals is the ability to recognize the brick walls life will place in front of you and climbing over those walls knowing that what you want is on the other side of that obstacle.

The wall isn't small nor is it easy to climb over but if you can sustain and gather the energy and effort to make it over you will be satisfied by what's on the other side of it.

To get over that hump means to operate in an uncomfortable environment and still excel. So by persevering, you'll become stronger and more comfortable with being uncomfortable.

Now the height of these walls vary from person to person, but the effort to get over the wall is the same. Anything less than 100% will get you up the wall and possibly to the top, but you will never get over it to the other side. 100% effort or more is what's required to make it to that other side.

On the other side, life takes on a new meaning as you begin to live above average. Understand this, living a life below or above average is a choice. We all have to face these obstacles and hit these walls. Your success is determined on your ability to either get over the wall or let the wall stop your progress. Your purpose for wanting to get to the other side needs to be much bigger than yourself in order for you to succeed and grow, if not I'm sure you'll quit.

Training Session 10
Graduation Day

"Did you realize that you were a champion in their eyes?"

~ Kanye West

"I'm so proud of you babe, my graduate!"

"It's not that big of a deal babe," I said to my girlfriend.

"It is a big deal to me; you worked hard for this accomplishment!"

"Ok... I guess you're right," I said in a monotone voice.

The reason for my nonchalant attitude was because of this, I graduated high school in 2008, and now it was 2015. Almost everyone that graduated with me in high school that attended college had already graduated from four-year institutes with their bachelors and some with their master's degrees, and here I was just getting my Associates Degree seven years later. I felt so far behind, and in a way I was insecure and embarrassed. Seven years wasted just to get two year degree? How could I waste this much time? Where did I go wrong? What was there to really be excited about?

As I went into the lobby to meet with the other graduates, I realized that what I viewed as embarrassing was a major accomplishment for everyone else. What really opened my eyes was that majority of the graduates were older than myself. Some of the graduates were old enough to be my parents, and they couldn't have been more excited to graduate today. Some graduates came with their kids, husbands, wives and even coworkers. They were excited as if they were graduating from Harvard. It was at that moment that I started to realize that when you finished didn't matter, but the fact that you persevered and finished is what really mattered. The fact that none of us quit was enough of a reason to celebrate. "We made it; we made it!" That's all I heard people screaming as they rejoiced. I paused for a second with a blank look on my face and realized that I made it as well. Through everything I encountered throughout my life I made it! I was offered the opportunity to quit and give up on myself a long time ago, but I didn't, and as a result of never quitting, I made it! This was a great start in creating a new appreciation of what I had accomplished. For years I would compare my life to others to see how I matched up and to see if I was winning or failing at life based on what everyone else was doing. Even though most of my friends graduated years ago and had careers I had to realize that we all had our own path in life and this was mines.

"Ok everyone the letters for each line are on the wall. Find the letter that matches your last name and line up," said the Dean of Students. As we began to line up and march to the gym where the ceremony was being held an overwhelming feeling had taken over my body as my mind shifted and I started to live in the moment. Something I've always dreamed of growing up was to have my mother clapping and screaming for me as I crossed a stage to be rewarded for a major accomplishment and now I was here, and that vision became a reality. As we marched from the main building on campus to the gymnasium I began to think about every obstacle life had put in my way for me to fail since I was a kid. My memory began to rewind back as I reminisced about my life over the last twenty-five years.

I bounced from house to house and parent to parent as a kid. I grew up in poverty and in the projects. I've been involved in gun shootings and drug transactions. I've lost friends to gang violence and drugs. My family was evicted from our home and almost homeless. I lost my best friend and grandfather to death. I went to nine different public schools and five different colleges, and I was close to committing suicide. These are just things that scratch the surface when it comes to issues I've faced in my life, and I still persevered to make it to this day of accomplishment. My girlfriend was right this was a big deal for me. This wasn't just a degree or a graduation; it was me choosing to live life and never give up on myself no matter what stood in my way or what my past looked like.

As we walked to the gymnasium, I could feel my eyes watering up with joy because I was finally finishing something after years of quitting and losing. I had finally won, and the people who mattered the most to me outside of my Pop Pop were there to witness and celebrate with me. As my name was called to walk up and grab my diploma I looked up, raised my left hand to the sky, pointed and said "I love you Pop-Pop" as a tear rolled down my cheek. It was as if I could hear my Pop-Pop bragging to all his friends back on Cedar Lane about me. I felt as if I had finally made him proud. I became a better person that day. A better version of myself was being created at that moment. A new chapter in my life was unfolding, and I was ready to embrace everything that came with it. No, this wasn't the initial goal of going to Memphis and getting a four-year degree, but it was a major goal, to say the least. By beating the odds stacked against me I now had opened a door for my younger brothers and future kids coming behind me as well as the following generations of kids coming up in my same environment and situations. They now would know what was possible if they too decided to never quit.

What most people didn't know about me was that my mission growing up was to go to the NBA and provide for my family. When that didn't work out I fell apart not even realizing that all of that adversity was preparing me for my true mission of inspiring and empowering those around me through my impact from adding value to their lives. When the mission was about myself and my hoop dreams I struggled and failed. Now that my mission was about others I felt as if I could do anything in the world and succeed without a doubt in my mind. I had seen myself as a loser and failure almost my whole life, but the people that supported me had seen me as a champion, and they always did I just never wanted to believe it.

Key #10 To Building Muscle:

You Only Fail If You Stop Trying.
You Can't Fail If You Never Quit

Training Session #11
To Be Continued…

*"When you learn to work from the inside out in
life, you understand your how, you understand your
why, and you understand your what!"*

~ Inky Johnson

"Say congratulations to the Class of 2015!" The Dean of Students said as we threw our caps to the ceiling in celebration of our commencement. It was a beautiful moment and one that I will never forget. I hadn't experienced this type of joy since I was younger during Christmas when the tree would be filled with gifts under it. I mean my mother was there, my great grandmother, my aunts, uncles, brother, best friends, and girlfriend. This was what winning felt like, and I instantly became addicted because of the pride I saw in the eyes of the people closest to me. I started receiving compliments and messages from people who were present during my personal storms about how proud they were of me and how inspired they were by my tolerance towards adversity and my courage to keep going even during the worst of times. Amid all this praise, I realized that I had a gift for motivating and inspiring others.

My journey was not about to stop at this accomplishment. This was just the beginning, and now I truly started to understand my purpose. This was the birth of me becoming a servant leader. Everyone who was there to celebrate my accomplishment and shared their love with me played a major role in helping me become the man I was today. It was time for me to impose my will and give those people who had invested their time and efforts into my life a return on their investment. It was time for me to serve and pour back into them and also the generations coming behind me. I was uncertain of my next step after graduation. I didn't know if I would continue going to school to receive my Bachelor's and Master's Degrees or if I would focus on branding my newfound passion for service, but whatever I decided to do I knew that I wouldn't quit because I had now set a new standard for my life.

I now viewed life in a different light because I knew on the other side of my struggles was a success. I was the kid that grew up poor eating syrup sandwiches and Top Ramen noodles more times than not. I was the kid who was made fun of. I was an insecure kid. I was the kid who lied to fit in. I've been through so much, and as a result of those situations I began to quit, and it became a domino effect throughout my entire life until now. I could have quit on my goal of getting a degree at any moment, I could have ended my life during those dark times, I could have kept my struggles and pain to myself, but I didn't, and that made me relatable, and it also propelled me to share my story with other people in similar situations that I've experienced and even some that I haven't. I wanted to show others that I built muscle and let them know that they can too if they persevere.

Key #11 To Building Muscle:

You Should Never Be The Main Focus Of Your Mission; The Focus Should Be On The Progression Of Others. That Is A Mission Worth Fighting For.

Stage 4 Review:

The most successful people in the world are in the business of helping others advance in life. Being selfless is the quickest and only guaranteed road to success.

Keys To Building Muscle #10-11

1. You Only Fail If You Stop Trying. You Can't Fail If You Never Quit.

2. You Should Never Be The Main Focus Of Your Mission; The Focus Should Be On The Progression Of Others. That Is A Mission Worth Fighting For.

Stage 5:

Someone Is Waiting On What You Are Building

Life has taught me that we as a human race are all entangled. Our life and how we live it directly affects others whether we believe it or not. I actually have a quote on my phone that I had since 2017 when I wrote my first book that says "Don't give up on your dream. Someone is waiting for what you're building." This simple yet powerful quote has served as a reminder to me that my dreams on which I am pursuing are not for my glory but for the empowerment of others.

The reason most people can quit on themselves as it pertains to their dreams and goals is that they have only seen how achieving such can benefit them and no one else. I once heard Dr. Eric Thomas say that someone asked him the question of "how do you wake up at 3 am and stay motivated?" His response was, "How did I start this presentation? With a picture of my wife and kids, duh it's easy stay motivated when you're not focused on you."

I've learned that even with the high expectations that I have for myself, I will take it easy and let myself down with little to no guilt. However, when I think of my brothers or my parents or even my future kids, I tap into another version of myself who doesn't believe or understand what quitting is. The pressure of letting someone else down is unbearable to me. It's a burden that I cannot handle and to avoid that burden I will do whatever is needed never to let my loved ones down. Even though they don't know that this is how I feel, I create imaginary emergencies in my head. The question of "what if" keeps me motivated to do better every single day. "What if my mom is diagnosed with a disease and can't afford her medical bills? What if my youngest brother needs help with his college tuition? What if my dad loses his job to an injury and can't afford his mortgage? What if my Wife wants to stay home with our future kid but can't take the year or two off because we can't afford it? I have so many different scenarios that I use, and they are there not to scare me but to keep a constant fire under me to stay motivated even when life throws more weight on me.

This motivation then allows me not just to be ready for those scenarios, but it also motivates me to keep building upon my dreams. I think about the laptop that I typed this book on. Someone owned their dream, and they were motivated to create the company that then created this laptop for me to own my dream and create this book which in turn will motivate and inspire someone else to own their dream and the cycle continues. Take the focus off of yourself. If you can keep those people whom you are building your dream for in your mind and heart especially when you want to quit, you will have the motivation you need to continue until the dream is fulfilled. On the flip side, if you only make your dream about you the chances of you quitting when things become difficult are dramatically increased. Being that you were put on this planet to fulfill your dreams, your life would be a waste if you didn't because of selfish pride and laziness. Also you would be robbing someone of the blessing that they needed from the offspring of your dream. NEVER QUIT, NEVER SETTLE! Your life is bigger than you.

Recovery Session
The Marathon Continues …

"The highest human act is to inspire"

~Nipsey Hussle

Life has trained me to see that when things are going wrong, people would rather work to make it look like nothing is wrong instead of working to fix what is wrong. That was my life's story shortly after my book release, which was about two years after my graduation from Atlantic Cape Community College. This is not to say that things were all bad, but I made sure to cover up the bad that was occurring as if it never happened. I went back into my closet and grabbed my mask of masculinity. My high from my previous graduation and my first book release wore off after all the praise left. I naively thought that just because I accomplished those things that life would instantly become beautiful and simplistic. I occurred some extreme lows right after those exciting highs of celebration. I thought that if I was nice to other people that they would respect me as an author, graduate and public speaker. I thought that if I offered my valuable time and effort to someone that they would not only appreciate it, but they would see me as a good person and reciprocate mutual energy. Unfortunately I was wrong. The cliche "nice guys finish last" had become my reality.

After my first book release for "BUILDING MUSCLE; LIFE IS YOUR TRAINER," I started to receive overwhelming support. People were taking pictures with the book, I was receiving direct messages from people on how the book impacted them, I was receiving emails about how great the book was, and I even received a few five-star reviews on Amazon from people who had purchased and read the book. I needed to continue the momentum if I wanted my story to continue to be shared and if I wanted BUILDING MUSCLE as a brand to grow. I became desperate for more exposure, and instead of staying focused on organically growing the brand through my grass-roots efforts and pouring into my loyal supporters, I started to seek help from people who I barely knew. I learned quickly that business is an aquarium full of fish and sharks run the show. I was vulnerable, and honestly I was easily influenced by others who seemed like they could help me take my business to the next level. I saw their lifestyle or at least the lifestyle that they allowed me to see and I took it for face value. If you had a nice car, business and could afford me as a personal trainer I assumed you had it all figured out.

After my first book signing event, I was certain that BUILDING MUSCLE would take off because of the incredible support. I also was going to school at Rowan University to pursue my Bachelors Degree. I was gaining momentum, and I finally felt like I was really breaking generational curses. I had already begun thinking of other venues and ideas to host another event. I deemed my first book signing event as the BUILDING MUSCLE EXPERIENCE. I envisioned my team and I traveling the east coast and then the country inspiring people to allow their life's experiences good or bad to make them stronger in all areas of their lives especially mentally. I wanted to serve others and speak with students in universities and high schools to empower them with tools that I learned throughout my years of struggling so that they could avoid those same painful struggles. I had a vision, and a purpose and I was ready to start this journey to inspire and heal. However I was still too vulnerable and naive. I became complacent, and I was basking in my social media success. The "likes" and "comments" were going to my head. I was killing it, or at least that was what it looked like. I looked like a successful author and excellent college student, but my bank account did not reflect that nor did my grades. I started to believe that my own flowers didn't stink, but the reality was that they were dead because I never watered them. I was too busy trying to look successful that I wasn't working to become successful.

I started to kill my own momentum. I second-guessed my dream and ultimately stayed stagnant for a few months. I had become frustrated with my lack of progress with my business and you could feel it within my aura. I even left school again. I began repeating the same bad habits of quitting on myself as I had previously done in the past. The chatterbox in my mind was winning every battle, and I downplayed everything I had done up until this point, and I discounted it to be some act of luck. I wasn't worthy of being a best-selling author, highly paid speaker and successful business owner. These were the thoughts that I would occasionally have throughout the day.

I felt lost and alone once again until I was approached to open my very own fitness studio not too far from my hometown. I never really had any real aspirations to open my own studio, but the picture of success painted by the individual who approached me seemed beautiful. I saw dollar signs, and I jumped on it without consulting with my Fiancee' or even having the money to actually properly open this fitness studio. I new this wasn't a sign from God to open this studio and leave school, but I justified it as such. I threw my dream in the backseat and replaced the passenger seat with a dream that someone else created for me. Long story short, my heart was never in it, and as a result my studio lasted for a total of three months before I officially closed its doors. I had sabotaged myself and put myself in a deep financial hole and even deeper depression. I had abandoned me and my Fiancee's plans to purchase our first home to open this studio. I had ignored my best friends concerns and placed my trust into someone who I assumed had my best interest at heart. I went from an extreme high the year before to a devastating low at that moment. I remember sitting in my car outside of the studio crying tears of pain and regret. How could I be so selfish? How could I be so careless? How did I even get to this point? I was supposed to be using my story to empower others, and I was supposed to graduate from Rowan University to continue a new legacy within my family. What I thought was a smart move to make a quick financial gain and bless those who invested in me and loved me ultimately turned around to punch me in the face with a Mike Tyson fist and run my pockets like a bully who wanted my lunch money.

Up until this point, I had done well with controlling my anxiety and depression, but I was beginning to lose that battle. Every day that followed the closing of my studio was more difficult than the day before. I had burned bridges when I opened my studio with people who truly supported me. Not only was my studio closed but I was broke, and no job would hire me. I was either over-qualified or under-qualified for my lack of schooling. I felt like an ex-con who couldn't even get a seasonal job. The month was November of 2018, and I was jobless, broken emotionally, mentally unstable, and my relationship with my Fiancee' was holding on by a thread. Everything in me wished that I could skip my birthday on December 13th and also Christmas because I felt as if I had nothing to celebrate and I didn't feel deserving of it. Also I knew that I could not afford gifts for anyone and I was ashamed to be in the position that I was in. The chatterbox in my mind became worse, and I would say demeaning things all day that I would never say to anyone else. That was how harsh my conversations with myself were. I started to hate myself and I concluded that I would forever live a life that was below mediocre. Self-talk can either kill you or help you live life abundantly. Most people don't understand that they are the voice that they hear in their minds. I was guilty of being one of those individuals from time to time. This occurred when I was in my darkest moments of my life.

Now I want to take this time to touch on a word that changed, better yet saved my life. That word is "obscurity," which means "to be obscured or hidden by darkness". See what I didn't understand was that during this time of obscurity, that during this dark time, I was building more muscle than I had ever built before and God was about to allow me to put my strength on display for the world!

Before my birthday in December, I was presented with an opportunity to talk about mental health and the effects of social media to a group of students and administrators at an EOF conference in Newark, NJ. The person who invited me had read my book and seen my story as value for their colleagues and students. This was something that I knew very well being that I experienced those devastating effects first hand when I tried to cover up my broken life with band-aids like posts of joy and success. Also I learned valuable lessons from those situations that ultimately helped my personal growth. That feeling of motivation that I once had when I graduated from Atlantic Cape Community College and started writing my first book started to return to me. Sharing my story with others made me feel a sense of purpose once again in my life. I loved every moment of it. I felt like a superhero, and my story was my superpower to save people. I then reclaimed my life from that boost of energy, and I went back to being fully accountable for my life and my decisions. I gathered the courage to go back to school. I changed my field of study to Liberal Studies which pertained directly to the work that I wanted my life's mission to reflect. As a 29-year-old student, it was easy for me to feel embarrassed or stupid but all of those feelings and thoughts of embarrassment no longer mattered. I was either going to change my behavior, or I was going to have to change my dream. I once heard Eric Thomas say that "Degrees don't say how long you've been in school or your age." All that matters is that you executed on graduating and that you would apply what you learned.

That initial speaking engagement that I had the pleasure to do then led to me speaking to the students of the residence life program at Morgan State University. I then was requested to come to Connecticut to share my testimony at a brunch conference. That then led to me speaking to 200+ students at Rutgers University Newark. The domino effect began to catch even more momentum as I was honored by Brookdale Community College as an honorary member of Chi Alpha Epsilon National Honor Society by someone that I met during my first speech at the EOF conference in Newark, NJ. Atlantic Cape Community College then honored me in front of my Fiancee', my best friend and his wife as one of the "Top 4 under 40 alumni." This was then proceeded by my graduation from Rowan University with a degree in Liberal Studies. I had completed more classes than I actually required during my extensive college journey starting at Lemoyne-Owen College in 2008 and as a result I only was required to take four classes before I would officially have my Bachelor's degree. God is funny sometimes, but he's right all the time if you follow the vision that he has for your life.

My parents have always heard me speak about the impact that I've wanted to make in the lives of others, but they've never had the actual opportunity to witness what that looks like. To them it may have looked like positive affirmations. It wasn't until I was asked by Atlantic Cape to speak during a scholarship award dinner for the upcoming school years award recipients and their donors that I was able to show my parents what my vision truly was instead of just telling them. My mother was first as she attended the award dinner with me. After I spoke and shared my experience at Atlantic Cape everyone in attendance was blown away by my oratory skills and my passionate message. Immediately after I left the stage my mother was swarmed by staff and students asking if she was my mother. They were giving her so much praise on my behalf, and I could see an overwhelming joy take over her being. That feeling of having my mother experience that praise and love was one of the best feelings I had ever experienced in my life. The amazing thing was that a week later I was able to recreate a similar experience but this time with my dad.

After the award dinner I was then asked to walk with the graduates of Atlantic Cape Community College class of 2019 as a Distinguished Alumni Member. My dad was approached by other students, and staff just like my mother was. They even gifted him some Atlantic Cape apparel as a thank you to me. It in many ways blew my mind that my dad who never went to college was being honored as if he did. Let's remember that my parents never attended college let alone graduated high school. As much as I was being celebrated and decorated, so were they. This was their graduation and accomplishments just as much as it was mines. They sacrificed finishing school for me, and I wanted to honor them for doing such. Maybe they never officially graduated from high school or college but they graduated with honors in the school of life and love. It's easy for me to accept my accomplishments as my own doing but the reality was that we had broke generational curses together. My life and this book you're reading is the proof of that.

I come from a family who didn't have a legacy. We were bound by poverty in our mindset, finances, and relationships. The beauty of life is that we have the opportunity to now create that legacy starting with me. Sometimes I sit and reflect on my life both past and present, and I wonder how many people needed to hear my story to learn how to BUILD MUSCLE in their own life. Selfish intentions will cause you to steal someone else's blessing. I challenge you to NEVER QUIT on your dreams because if nothing else, someone is waiting on what you're building.

Epilogue

Hard work is cute, but execution is all that matters. I use to be the guy who always wanted the knowledge but did nothing with it. I watched all the motivational videos on YouTube, I listened to all the podcasts on becoming a success, operating a business and writing a book. The issue wasn't my lack of knowledge or resources the issue was my lack of execution. Throughout these trials that I discuss in this book I "Built Muscle" and I became an executor. My goal for this book is to not just speak about my flaws for sympathy because that doesn't matter to me but instead my goal is to pass on the lessons that life taught me. I want those lessons to help others drive around those same roadblocks that I once stopped at. I want people to understand that they are not alone in how they are feeling. This isn't just a book but a guide to building a strong unbreakable mentality by using your own experiences with life as your personal trainer to build the life that you've always wanted. Every loss isn't a failure but it is a chance to learn a lesson so don't run from a loss or let them discourage you.

What I want the reader to understand is that even though in this book I provided keys that helped me grow into the man I am today, those keys only matter if you apply them and then teach them to others. That's what I define as living your best life. The real blessing is in blessing others and not just receiving. I want to leave you with this; you have no limits on how much muscle you can build, you're in control. Life will continue to supply the weight, but it's up to you to lift it. What started out with me just wanting to share my story has now become a part of my life's work. Let's continue BUILDING MUSCLE together!

With Love and Gratitude

~ Nate

Book Nathan Evans Jr.

Nathan Evans Jr. is known for his motivational and inspiring presence in person and on social media as well as being a highly requested inspirational speaker and fitness trainer. He has become a public figure and servant leader within his community. His message, along with his passion, has inspired thousands of students across the country and he's showing no signs of slowing down.

- Author

- Inspirational speaker

- Distinguished Alumni of ACCC

- Honorary member of Chi Alpha Epsilon National Honor Society

- Mentor

- Mental health advocate

- Award-winning personal trainer

Contact Nathan Evans Jr.

Email for booking: info@nateevansjr.com

Website: www.nateevansjr.com

Follow Nathan Evans Jr.

Instagram: www.instagram.com/nate.evansjr

Twitter: www.twitter.com/nate_evansjr

Facebook: www.facebook.com/nathanevansjr

LinkedIn: www.linkedin.com/in/nathan-evans-jr-ba5a4664

Made in the USA
Middletown, DE
18 January 2020

83033793R00061